THE CROSSFIT JOURNEY

HOW TO BE A HEALTHY CROSSFITTER AND HOW TO AVOID INJURY

EricK M. McKenney

Contents

Chapter One

INTRODUCTION

You've probably failed several times previously. But that's okay; many others, including myself, have done the same thing. It's not always simple to see the light at the end of the tunnel. After all, it took me years of being incorrect before I realized I was correct. You either win or you learn, that's the way it works. There's no term for 'loss' in my dictionary. I'm sure, like me, you've been at a fork in the road. You chose this book for a purpose. The only difference is that I had no idea what was blocking my route, so I had to piece everything together slowly and painstakingly.

My exercise plan was ineffective. My sleeping patterns were off. I didn't even have a food plan that was specifically tailored to my needs. I couldn't find the perfect platform to learn what I needed to know to make things right since I was living life in the fast lane, pursuing goal after dream and being engulfed by unending responsibilities...until I did.

2   THE CROSSFIT JOURNEY

It's one thing to see a problem and be unsure of what to do about it; it's another to be unsure whether an issue exists at all. For example, I had no idea how my frantic lifestyle was producing a mental overload or how my haphazard exercise routine was leading to injury. I was fortunate enough to learn before it was too late, and I did get lucky on occasion. However, this isn't true for everyone. That's why I'm going to show you how you can be setting yourself up for failure without you realizing it, as well as the steps you can take to change things and become a great CrossFit athlete.

Chapter Two

JURIE COMMON CAUSES OF WORK

We're so fixated on achieving milestones that we forget about the effort required to get there. That's how I remember my first CrossFit effort.

There is always space for improvement, that is an irrefutable reality. It doesn't matter whether you've been doing this for years or if you're brand new to the game and still learning the ropes—the risk of being hurt is always there.

Granted, individuals who have gotten the hang of it are less likely to sustain an injury, but there are a number of other considerations to consider. Mistakes, poor judgments, and a general lack of attention may all lead to regretful outcomes. Those who have been wounded during an exercise, such as yourself, will understand how much it costs. Knowing how much it costs, on the other hand, does not always imply that you know what it takes to prevent it from occurring again. There is no such thing as being too cautious.

4   THE CROSSFIT JOURNEY

I wasn't a big fan of gymnastics or any other type of athleticism until a few years ago. In fact, being in my comfort zone appealed to me more than anything else. When my friends and I agreed to meet up for a fun soccer game on a lovely summer day, though, I found that both sides were hesitant to have me on their squad. It was a wake-up call for me, despite the fact that it was nothing major. The insight prompted me to reflect on and evaluate earlier instances in which I had been seen as the weak link when it comes to physical pursuits. I was alright as long as I made the choice to not participate in sports on my own, but the fact that others began to believe I lacked the necessary skills began to wear me down. Suddenly, there was an obsession.

As a result, I grew adamant—despite the fact that I was still dumb. The good news was that I had finally developed a desire to make this life-altering change. After all, it had taken such a long time. I had no notion where to begin, which was the bad news. I went online, just like the typical Joe, to ask the most basic inquiries and see what other internet users had to say about it. That's when I discovered High-Intensity Interval Training (HIIT) (also known as HIIT). That piqued my interest the most out of all I'd read. Later on, I learned more about CrossFit training, which is not just a kind of high-intensity interval training but also a training philosophy. I went from being a gym skeptic to a walking encyclopedia.

When it came time to apply what I'd learned in class to my everyday life, I was all set. Just to have a place to practice, I promptly enrolled in a CrossFit training program. My desire to succeed was soaring. I was ecstatic, and I believed I could outperform anybody with similar objectives.

I hurt my lower back after just a few weeks of consistent workout.

It turns out that my enthusiasm had blinded me to all that truly mattered in terms of my own safety. This was a significant setback for me, but it did not spell the end of my CrossFit quest. I made up my decision right then and there: with a long road ahead of me, now was not the time to call it quits and abandon all that had brought me to this point. So I went back to square one, attempting to determine what had gone wrong the previous time. As I previously said, you either win or learn; my initial effort yielded the latter.

Whether you've been there or not, I can assure you that you must take care of your body in addition to training it. Workout injuries are prevalent, but they may be avoided with the right precautions. At the very least, several interrelated aspects that may all be classed under one umbrella—your well-being—can significantly reduce the total risks associated with exercise injuries.

MORE DOESN'T ALWAYS equate to better.

CrossFit is, in my opinion, more of an art form than a kind of exercise. It's referred to as "the sport of fitness" in philosophical terms. It's something you comprehend, consume, and experience. Expect to take a long time to improve if you want to be excellent at it. Putting in more effort doesn't always imply that you'll be better than the competition. CrossFit isn't just about speed, which may come as a surprise to some. One heartbeat at a time, you take it slowly. You repeat this process until the 'new' has become 'normal.' Even if you're sweating profusely at the conclusion of your exercise, it doesn't mean it was a success. Unless you want to sweat a lot.

When the goal is to make money, you put in long hours every day. However, keep in mind that this is one of the most common blunders. The process of seeing results takes time. Unfortunately, most of us lack the patience necessary to deal with such a concept. Before you do anything else, you should be able to recognize when it is time to stop. Endurance training is a physically demanding process. And, like everyone else, you have boundaries. While pushing those boundaries may seem like a motivating thought, there are productive and responsible ways to do so. "Rome wasn't built in a day," as the proverb goes. When you repeat the same routine over and over and don't see results, you'll feel frustrated, but don't let it cloud your judgment.

"What have I got to lose?" you might think. So, what's the answer to that? It's all about you. It's perfectly fine to skip one or more days of your workout routine. It is not acceptable to make up for it the next day by going above and beyond. Also, don't be the weekend warrior who crams everything into two days instead of taking his or her time to create a well-balanced schedule. You'll be torturing yourself without realizing it if you don't keep your balance. You may have heard of overnight successes, but athleticism defies logic. Simply put, when you know it's time to stop, you know it's time. Don't be surprised if something bad happens if you keep going, believing nothing bad will happen.

The problem is that some of us are born with more natural strength than others. Some of us believe we can accomplish more during our regular workout sessions. You can work twice as hard as the rest of the team and still be satisfied at the end of the day. However, working out, like everything else, has limits. The more you push yourself beyond those limits, the more likely you are to get hurt. Consider your body as a metaphorical machine to solve the problem mentioned previously. It's the same as driving a car for as long as you want until it breaks down, at which point the term "forever" becomes meaningless. Your body will have no choice but to give up in some shape or form if pressure and stress are applied consistently. As a result, work even harder than you have been, but never more than you should.

HEALTHFULNESS

It's crucial to eat right. It is, without a doubt, one of the most important aspects of your overall health. Even if you don't exercise, being well-nourished is essential for good health. It's even more important as an athlete, and this is a well-known fact. It's a simple rule: eat to stay healthy. Just because you've spent a lot of time at the gym or at the fitness center doesn't mean you're ready. This was also one of my rookie mistakes when I first began my CrossFit journey, speaking from personal experience. It took a drop in my performance for me to notice the issue, and then there was the problem of figuring out how to fix it. You must pay attention to what goes into your body in addition to the physical activities that you engage in.

Muscles break when you exercise, and this can happen with almost any exercise. Have you ever had that stingy feeling after breaking your own record for the most push-ups in a single go? That's your body telling you that your muscles have suffered tissue damage and need to be repaired. This is entirely reasonable. Following this occurrence, your body seeks out nutritional elements to aid in the healing process. It seeks out high-protein sources in particular. Both before and after the workout, your body must be properly nourished and hydrated. If you work out hard but don't pay attention to your body's needs, you'll almost certainly lose rather than gain.

This does not, however, imply that you are free to take whatever is on the menu with you. Food is important, but the type of food you consume is even more crucial. To put it another way, what you eat is who you are. This phrase has a lot of meaning, but it's literal in the fitness world. You can't expect your body to be in good shape if you eat unhealthy foods after a vigorous workout. Eating unhealthy foods can be just as harmful to your health as not eating any at all. Sugary and fatty foods are frequently linked to bone loss, muscle loss, and other health problems. Your body will suffer if it is not supported properly. If you don't eat well, you'll notice that your workout performance suffers. In addition, if you perform poorly, you're more likely to get hurt. A bad diet cannot be out-executed.

Chapter Three

THE DANGER SOF SLEEP DEPRIVATION

Back in 2019, I had become a fitness enthusiast in every sense of the word. Not only that, I was arguably in my best shape throughout the course of my life. Fitness apart, I also had a\sbig corporate presentation coming up that was to be held overseas. My colleagues and I had been working on a startup project which had caught the eyes of an angel investor. We were all stoked about it, but it was a lot of work. There was simply no way we could mess it up. We spent weeks prepping for it, and, during those weeks, my work schedule became hard to cope with—it started eating up portions from the non-work-related side of my life. I, being a fitness freak, could not imagine taking a break from the training, especially when I knew for a fact that I was the best shape I had ever been in. So, I started pulling all-nighters, trying to find the smallest of gaps to fit my fitness schedule in (pun intended) (pun intended).

For a month or so, I can safely say that I was sleeping for about 2 to 3 hours a night at best . I was downright happy with what I was doing; I didn't have to compromise my professional obligations or my fitness routine. However, what I was compromising, unknowingly, was my health.

So, my colleagues and I were all waiting for the big day. We had prepped and rehearsed everything. Our flights had been booked. Being perfectionists, having even the slightest margin for error was out of the question. We had eliminated every single problem that we could forecast. Then, the unexpected happened. About 2 days before our flight, I realized that my limbs, specifically my arms, were twitching. I was fine, but the waves of intermittent vibrations I felt were something that I had never before experienced. I shrugged it off and went to bed that night. The next morning, I had absolutely no feeling in my arms and legs. They had gone numb.

Anxiety had taken a toll on me, with the root cause being sleep deprivation. I was immediately concerned. It wasn't something I could afford from either a professional or an athletic point of view. I was able to walk, but not like normal people do. I remember having to crawl out (literally) of bed that morning to get ready for work. It was no different than one of those cliché scenes in an action movie where the protagonist is trying to grab their gun during the last moments of their life to save the world, or, well, at least themselves.

I was in no shape to drive to work, so I called for help. The thing is, I didn't understand why any of it was happening. For the first half of the day, my colleagues and I were still looking at the situation from a humorous perspective. We decided to visit a doctor in the afternoon, though. They ran some tests, which indicated that something big was going to come out of them. The doctor then proceeded to sit me down, looked me dead in the eye, and said, "You're sleep- deprived."

Although it was a relief to hear that I wasn't attacked by some killer mutation that suddenly

took control of half of my body, it was also unpleasant to hear how careless I had been about my body for a month or so. When they said what they said, it all made sense. They didn't have to break it down for me or explain it. Deep down, I did know that I just hadn't been getting enough sleep for God-knows-how-long. No wonder my performance at the training center during those days were not as good as they usually were. No wonder I was unable to focus on the simplest of things at times. The doctor told me that it was nothing to worry about and that I just needed to get enough sleep so that my limbs would start functioning normally once the effects of the stress are gone. That also meant that I would have to limp my way around for the next couple of days or so.

Ultimately, exercising was out of the question. I could barely walk without losing balance. I wasn't allowed to stress myself any further. Not being able to train was a heavy blow for me. Then, there was all the uncertainty about the upcoming presentation that could not be postponed; I didn't want to back out of it, either. It was weeks and weeks of relentless work that had led up to that moment, after all. So, we went forward with it. The most embarrassing thing for me was the fact that my colleagues had to carry my bags during the trip because my hands would just give up as soon as I tried to lift any weight. Being the fittest person in the room, I never imagined there would come a day when I would ask someone to carry my bag; a bag that contained nothing but a laptop, a charger, some protein bars, and a notebook.

Behavioral Changes

When you're sleep-deprived, one of the instant giveaways is a decline in your mood. You'll see yourself becoming short-tempered towards things that you would otherwise be okay with. Getting irritated or agitated by situations that don't deserve such a reaction is never a sign of good health. If you're physically fit but mentally worn out, then you're just not fit. Sleep deprivation obstructs the way your brain cells communicate with each other, and this occurrence will adversely affect your psychological state. If you're someone who suffers from anxiety or stress-related disorders, then this could be all the more dangerous for you. Be on the lookout for any abrupt mood swings. Try to identify the problem before it worsens and affects your daily life.

Fatigue

Being fatigued is perhaps the earliest or most common sign that you'll get when you're suffering from insufficient sleep. If you've just begun your day and are already yawning like you've been up for an eternity, then you're likely sleep-deprived. During workouts, you will also notice that your muscles are just not responding the way they normally. The more fatigued you are, the more drastically your workouts will be affected. When you're in such a state, it's never a good idea to involve yourself in challenging exercises. The coordination between your brain and your body will just not be in its best form. You may think to yourself that you'll endure it because, perhaps, you've done it a thousand times before. But your body will just not be able to bear it.

Lack of Energy during Workouts

As a combination of every other factor that will indicate your sleep deprivation, one of the most obvious things that you'll come to notice is how quickly you'd be getting tired from the exercises you normally do. The urge to stop will set in much faster than it usually does, leaving you in an exhausted state. When this happens, you can bet that your body hasn't had enough sleep, and thus its potential to withstand the exercise has been negatively influenced. Partaking in exercises characterized by a high degree of intensity without having the right amount of energy to contend is the equivalent of contesting in a game of tug of war where your teammates suddenly decide to back out one by one. You're bound to fail eventually.

CONSEQUENCES OF SLEEP DEPRIVATION

The signs, if left untreated, can turn into effects that will harm you in numerous ways. It shouldn't come as a surprise, as anything that's left to overload is bound to break one way or another. Your body is not immune to the effects of sleep deprivation, no matter what age group you belong to. Truth be told, several studies suggest that the lack of sufficient sleep can cause many medical conditions that can shorten a person's overall life expectancy. Simply put, if sleep deprivation goes on for long, it can kill you. Albeit being a destructive process that takes its time, you will see some of the relatively alarming consequences start to show up if you keep pushing yourself without caring about the rest time your body deserves. The worst part? Some of these consequences may cause irreversible damage.

Poor Judgment and Memory

It's also no hidden fact that sleep deprivation affects the way you think. Or, more straightforwardly put, it makes you dumb. There's no better way of saying it. It's a combination of negative factors that contribute to a person's dumbness when he or she has made a lifestyle out of sleeping insufficiently. Sleep deprivation will reduce cognitive functioning ability, which in turn will make it harder for you to understand and utilize information. Your brain's ability to get a grasp on things will be delayed. Moreover, sleep deprivation will also lower your power to memorize things. You will start to forget more frequently than you once did. This will only worsen with time if you don't take action.

Resemblance with Concussions

The scariest—albeit the most interesting—detail of the matter is that people who suffer from prolonged sleep deprivation and those who suffer from concussions have almost the same kind of symptoms. Memory loss, poor judgment, mood swings, confusion, and more, are all effects that a person faces in sleep deprivation as well as during a concussion. Just by seeing the intensity of these effects, you can tell how important sleep is for the average human being if the goal is a healthy lifestyle. Think about it this way—concussions are normally caused by physical blows to the head, where a person is directly hurt. Hence, in that case, the persona at least sees it coming. Now, if sleep deprivation can do the same damage without any direct blow, always remaining behind the curtains, its danger is explicit.

Chapter Four

STRESS ND DANXIETY: THE STEALTHY KILLER

Let's face it. Stress and anxiety have become part of our daily lives. Even the most self- contained people go through it. In fact, some of us suffer from stress and anxiety without even realizing. Without an official diagnosis, many of us may not be able to tell the difference between ordinary mood swings and underlying anxiety disorders. What I can assure you, however, is that the latter is no joke. Stress and anxiety have been labeled as the fuel to the fire that burns down an average person's life. They will take birth inside you, reside within you, and damage you without you realizing until it's too late. So, if you don't intend to do something about it, I can assure you that having an unsuccessful CrossFit career will be the least of your problems.

Stress is often referred to as the "Stealthy Killer". They call it that because, unlike other diseases, you don't see the vivid effects when stress is taking your life. Nowadays, stress can be triggered by events that don't necessarily have a tragic story tied to them. It's all about your emotions and how you feel as a person. That is also why it's so easy to overlook stress in ourselves as well as others. One of the most wrong assumptions that people make when they see others smiling or laughing is that they're happy. People who suffer from stress or anxiety will not show obvious signs. They might suffer without even knowing it, and hence be just like us when we see them. Under the lid, there will be a war being waged that nobody will know about. Perhaps not even the victim.

The unfortunate part about all of this is that stress is inevitable. The human body is designed in such a way that it automatically retrieves stress according to the situations it is put in. As a kid, I used to get very tense whenever the exam season was close. A sense of discomfort would gradually build up inside, making me unable to enjoy what I would be doing. I know for a fact that most kids go through the same thing, and although it's something ordinary, it can serve as perhaps a low-scale example of how stress can build up inside us. Now, as an adult, having a much better understanding of how all of it works, I can undoubtedly say that most of us do get stressed from our jobs. It's not that you don't necessarily love what you do for a living, but it's more about how we take it in.

Despite leading an amazing professional life, circumstances at my workplace every now and then have caused me to become mentally exhausted. As someone who doesn't take vacation breaks due to an overtly insistent sense of ownership, I sometimes suffer from the backfiring when push comes to shove. When I have too much on my plate, other parts of my life are bound to be affected. And yes, there have been many times when I was in the workout room with absolutely no idea of what I was doing. It's okay if that happens to you. The important thing is to remember how to not lose control and to keep balance. As an athlete, being strong is not enough. You have to be equally smart.

Speaking of smart, when you're in the middle of your workout, you have to keep a tab on the pointers that may affect your performance. This requires you to always be conscientious before anything else. For instance, knowing about how stress can have a negative impact on your health, if you ever find yourself confused or dazed inside the workout area, consider that as a red flag. As a smart CrossFit athlete, you should know when to stop. Just like it was said above—and I can't stress this enough—your body will always send you signals for anything that bothers it. At the end of the day, it's up to you and your ability to recognize that your workout is affected, and then track down the problem before it turns into a disaster.

NEGATIVE IMPACTS

Just like sleep deprivation, untreated stress can put you in serious trouble. I wouldn't be exaggerating if I told you that the negative impacts of stress are far worse than what you may have to deal with from sleep deprivation. After all, sleep deprivation is one of the causes of stress, which also means that stress is something that you would experience on an advanced level when the aforementioned occurs. Paint a picture in your mind with a hierarchy that puts stress above most of the other reasons why you might fail as an athlete. Like I've emphasized before, it's much better for you to stop, take a break, re-strategize, and get back up rather than keep pushing yourself to the peaks of destruction just to reach a certain milestone. The price you'll pay for stress damage is just too much for what it gives—and it's not worth it.

Slow Recovery

Stress can occupy your body's functions so much that it hinders your recovery after a workout. Like we discussed before, after an intensive workout, your body needs recovery for the best kinds of results, and recovery is obtained through nutrition and rest. There is a phase right after your workout when your body expects the resources it depends on for its recovery. Stress can multiply how worn out you feel after a workout and delay the recovery altogether. Then, when you're empty-tanked, it will also be harder for you to find the right amount of energy to get yourself ready for the next workout. If you're stubborn and you still push for it, you'll just be putting yourself in danger. Without appropriate recovery, workouts can harm your body rather than benefit it.

OVERCOMING STRESS AND ANXIETY

Seeing that stress and anxiety can become such huge issues for your workout lifestyle, it needs no convincing that they need to be addressed. For starters, what you can do is try to analyze your current lifestyle to see what needs some tweaking. Forget about your goals for a moment. Try to focus more on what isn't going your way. There are techniques that can be used to implement balance in one's life. If you're not happy with what you're doing, then either you're doing it wrong, or you shouldn't be doing it at all. But it's different for every individual. Before jumping to conclusions, you should take your time to recognize and analyze everything with a calm mind. When you get the gut feeling that something is harming you, it most likely is.

Well-balanced Eating

Chapter Five

YOUR BODY AND BRAINARE STARVING

4

Day in and day out, you probably put in a lot of time at the gym. You've done your homework, devised a fantastic exercise regimen, and have all the virtual energy you'll ever need to go out there and be the best version of yourself. Despite this, you're having trouble. You put in a lot of effort to push yourself past your limits, but you don't always see any results. To make matters worse, when you do, they aren't exactly what you had hoped for. It begins to feel as if everything you do is futile.

As a result, you change things up. Perhaps you push yourself even harder, or you switch up the types of workouts you do to see if the change improves your results. After a few weeks or months, you realize none of it has worked out. If you find yourself in this situation, you're probably overlooking one of the most important aspects of being a successful athlete: your diet.

Let's start with one of the most common misunderstandings about the term "diet." No, just because you're on a diet doesn't mean you have to live on salad and goat food. Diet can refer to a number of things. It's more of a case-by-case recommendation than a broad recommendation. As you can see, some people gain weight more quickly than others. Some people have a difficult time losing weight, while others never gain weight regardless of what they eat. It has to do with your body's many functions, particularly your metabolism. That is why bodies are divided into categories. As an ectomorph, I had no idea how important it was for me to eat the right foods in order to see good results at first. I was under the impression that if I just gave it my all inside the training center while eating a veggie-pro diet, everything would be fine. It didn't work out.

Yes, I began to notice a more defined shape to my body, but this occurred without me gaining any significant weight. To begin with, I was a frail individual. So, months later, I was a well-defined skinny person after a strenuous workout routine with no regard for diet. That wasn't the objective I had in mind. I became dissatisfied with my workout results and began looking in all directions for any miraculous tips or advice that could drastically alter the course of my workout life. I became reliant on the opinions of others in the gym, particularly those who were in excellent physical condition. In the process, I completely overlooked the fact that what works for one person may not work for another. To put it another way, each body's requirements differ.

Without a doubt, copying what others around me were doing and applying it to myself was a rookie mistake. Our bodies are built in different ways. Our bodies change as we age, and our cravings change as well. There is no linear solution to a person's dietary problem; eating more or less is not the answer. The key to success is finding the right balance for you. This, in particular, necessitates patience. If you want to be influenced, the very least you can do is make sure the person you're getting ideas from has a body type similar to yours and shares your goals. Even then, though, it's a stab in the dark. A fish will never ask a bird for instructions on how to fly. I thought that stuffing myself with food three times a day (until I couldn't breathe any longer) would solve the problem, but it only made things worse.

More importantly, when you do high-intensity workouts, your body looks to you to compensate for the calories you burn. Consider your body as a car ready to put in some serious miles on a road trip along the California coast. You've got everything planned out except the fuel. So, what's next? You become stranded in the middle of your journey, and your journey comes to a halt. Use the same logic when it comes to your workout routine. You want to get buff, or you want to lose weight—whatever your goal is, your body requires that fuel to function. You'll hit a brick wall if you don't have it. In high-intensity workouts, your body will require even more resources to recover. If you don't give it to yourself, your recovery will be hampered, and you'll notice that you're losing muscle, which is never a good sign.

Regardless of your workout routine, your body requires care and attention. A human being must be fed in order to give their absolute best. Throughout your life, your body and brain require a variety of resources of various sizes and types. However, if you put your body to a lot of work, the requirements may change. When it comes to food, there is no bypass for people like us who have made exercising a way of life. As a result, it is critical for any athlete to maintain a consistent monitoring of their eating patterns, as failing to do so will only cause you to suffer.

WHAT HAPPENS TO YOUR BODY AND BRAIN

Malnutrition can lead to abnormal brain development. To dispel some misconceptions about malnutrition, it is not only a problem that affects infants and children as they grow older. Malnutrition can strike at any time in your life, including adulthood. People who work out or want to work out, like you, are not immune to suffering. Specifically, if you stop caring about your diet and focus solely on the part of burning the fuel, you will gradually become deficient in the nutrients required to maintain a healthy brain. A lack of certain nutrients can hasten the loss of neurons in your brain, affecting your abilities such as coordination, memorization, and even speech.

But first, let's define malnutrition in more detail. Is it a medical condition? No. Is it a disease that develops as a result of nutrient deficiency or excessive consumption? Absolutely. "Wait a minute!" you might be thinking. How does overeating cause malnutrition? Isn't it supposed to be the other way around?" That is precisely the point. Malnutrition affects both men and women. You'll most likely suffer from malnutrition whether you're underweight or obese.

Your body now sends you signals that you are malnourished when you reach the highest point on the scale or the lowest point on the scale. In other words, you will begin to notice symptoms before it becomes apparent that a problem is about to occur. Malnutrition is characterized by a lack of appetite and a sudden loss of interest in eating. So, even if you haven't eaten anything, your body won't be as hungry as it should be. This, in turn, will cause a slew of minor but noticeable issues, such as a lack of concentration, fatigue, muscle loss, and even depression. You simply cannot afford to let your brain or body suffer if you have workout-related goals to meet, milestones to cross, and so on.

It's also no secret that malnutrition can harm you in ways that are considered critical to your health in the long run. Undernutrition, for example, can lead to obesity and heart disease later in life. Although you may not notice these diseases right away, the underlying changes in your body will orchestrate you down the path of damage. A good example of such changes is your metabolism, which will be drastically altered if you are undernourished. You can't expect anything good to come out of your workout routine when your body is being harmed in the worst way possible. So, unless organ failure is a long-term goal, you should think carefully about what you put into your body.

FOOD AND HIIT

Your body should get the food it needs to operate while you're exercising before you start working out—ideally, one to three hours before. Carbohydrates and protein should make up the majority of this.

Because carbohydrates burn quickly, they are deemed more important in this case. In other words, they provide a quick source of energy. Yes, carbs have a bad rep in the workout world, but it's a little-known fact that they're the best kind of resource for providing your body with enough fuel. Bananas, peanut butter toasts, and Greek yogurt are some of the most popular pre-workout foods among regular exercisers. There are probably more combinations out there, but as long as your body gets the right amount of energy from what you eat, you'll be fine.

When it comes to carbohydrates, keep in mind that not all carbs have the same effect on your body. Simple carbohydrates and complex carbohydrates are the two types of carbohydrates. Simple carbs are carbs that are easily broken down and absorbed, for an easy comparison between the two. Because quick absorption is a result of rapid digestion, it's safe to assume that simple carbohydrates are digested more quickly. Fruit juice concentrate, white bread, and milk are examples of simple carbohydrates. Complex carbs, on the other hand, are a different story. These carbs, as you may have guessed, take a long time to break down. They endure longer within your body, providing a steady supply of energy. On the cover, it appears that complex carbs are the way to go for better workout results. However, you don't want to find yourself in a scenario where your body is left behind.

Pre-workout meals should include a well-balanced mix of simple and complex carbohydrates for balance.

Let us now turn our attention to protein. Is it true that carbs are all you need before a workout? No, that is not the case. Protein is just as important for the post-workout phase of your body as carbs are for the pre-workout phase. Because protein is essential for recovery and because HIIT may cause minor muscle injury, your bloodstream should be stocked with enough protein to leap into action as soon as you leave the gym. It's good to incorporate some protein in your pre-workout meal, but not to the point where you feel too full to exercise afterwards. If you're going to have a protein-rich meal, it's best to avoid doing so shortly before your workout. Protein, unlike carbohydrates, takes longer to digest.

Your meal should be timed to coincide with the amount of time until you start your workout. When you just have a few minutes to spare, it's never a smart idea to consume anything that won't be digested in that time. This is why sports drinks exist for athletes who want to gain energy quickly without having to worry about the details. Water is one of the other essentials that your body requires prior to, during, and after your workout. In the realm of workouts, hydration is sometimes forgotten. It should come as no surprise that optimal hydration is responsible for a slew of little details that add up to a big influence on your exercise. Your body will sweat throughout your exercise, which will cause you to lose water. To avoid dehydration during your workout, make sure you have enough water in your tank.Day in and day out, you probably put in a lot of time at the gym. You've done your homework, devised a fantastic exercise regimen, and have all the virtual energy you'll ever need to go out there and be the best version of yourself. Despite this, you're having trouble. You put in a lot of effort to push yourself past your limits, but you don't always see any results. To make matters worse, when you do, they aren't exactly what you had hoped for. It begins to feel as if everything you do is futile. As a result, you change things up. Perhaps you push yourself even harder, or you switch up the types of workouts you do to see if the change improves your results. After a few weeks or months, you realize none of it has worked out. If you find yourself in this situation, you're probably overlooking one of the most important aspects of being a successful athlete: your diet.

Let's start with one of the most common misunderstandings about the term "diet." No, just because you're on a diet doesn't mean you have to live on salad and goat food. Diet can refer to a number of things. It's more of a case-by-case recommendation than a broad recommendation. As you can see, some people gain weight more quickly than others. Some people have a difficult time losing weight, while others never gain weight regardless of what they eat. It has to do with your body's many functions, particularly your metabolism. That is why bodies are divided into categories. As an ectomorph, I had no idea how important it was for me to eat the right foods in order to see good results at first. I was under the impression that if I just gave it my all inside the training center while eating a veggie-pro diet, everything would be fine. It didn't work out.

Yes, I began to notice a more defined shape to my body, but this occurred without me gaining any significant weight. To begin with, I was a frail individual. So, months later, I was a well-defined skinny person after a strenuous workout routine with no regard for diet. That wasn't the objective I had in mind. I became dissatisfied with my workout results and began looking in all directions for any miraculous tips or advice that could drastically alter the course of my workout life. I became reliant on the opinions of others in the gym, particularly those who were in excellent physical condition. In the process, I completely overlooked the fact that what works for one person may not work for another. To put it another way, each body's requirements differ.

Without a doubt, copying what others around me were doing and applying it to myself was a rookie mistake. Our bodies are built in different ways. Our bodies change as we age, and our cravings change as well. There is no linear solution to a person's dietary problem; eating more or less is not the answer. The key to success is finding the right balance for you. This, in particular, necessitates patience. If you want to be influenced, the very least you can do is make sure the person you're getting ideas from has a body type similar to yours and shares your goals. Even then, though, it's a stab in the dark. A fish will never ask a bird for instructions on how to fly. I thought that stuffing myself with food three times a day (until I couldn't breathe any longer) would solve the problem, but it only made things worse.

More importantly, when you do high-intensity workouts, your body looks to you to compensate for the calories you burn. Consider your body as a car ready to put in some serious miles on a road trip along the California coast. You've got everything planned out except the fuel. So, what's next? You become stranded in the middle of your journey, and your journey comes to a halt. Use the same logic when it comes to your workout routine. You want to get buff, or you want to lose weight—whatever your goal is, your body requires that fuel to function. You'll hit a brick wall if you don't have it. In high-intensity workouts, your body will require even more resources to recover. If you don't give it to yourself, your recovery will be hampered, and you'll notice that you're losing muscle, which is never a good sign.

Regardless of your workout routine, your body requires care and attention. A human being must be fed in order to give their absolute best. Throughout your life, your body and brain require a variety of resources of various sizes and types. However, if you put your body to a lot of work, the requirements may change. When it comes to food, there is no bypass for people like us who have made exercising a way of life. As a result, it is critical for any athlete to maintain a consistent monitoring of their eating patterns, as failing to do so will only cause you to suffer.

WHAT HAPPENS TO YOUR BODY AND BRAIN

Malnutrition can lead to abnormal brain development. To dispel some misconceptions about malnutrition, it is not only a problem that affects infants and children as they grow older. Malnutrition can strike at any time in your life, including adulthood. People who work out or want to work out, like you, are not immune to suffering. Specifically, if you stop caring about your diet and focus solely on the part of burning the fuel, you will gradually become deficient in the nutrients required to maintain a healthy brain. A lack of certain nutrients can hasten the loss of neurons in your brain, affecting your abilities such as coordination, memorization, and even speech.

But first, let's define malnutrition in more detail. Is it a medical condition? No. Is it a disease that develops as a result of nutrient deficiency or excessive consumption? Absolutely. "Wait a minute!" you might be thinking. How does overeating cause malnutrition? Isn't it supposed to be the other way around?" That is precisely the point. Malnutrition affects both men and women. You'll most likely suffer from malnutrition whether you're underweight or obese.

Your body now sends you signals that you are malnourished when you reach the highest point on the scale or the lowest point on the scale. In other words, you will begin to notice symptoms before it becomes apparent that a problem is about to occur. Malnutrition is characterized by a lack of appetite and a sudden loss of interest in eating. So, even if you haven't eaten anything, your body won't be as hungry as it should be. This, in turn, will cause a slew of minor but noticeable issues, such as a lack of concentration, fatigue, muscle loss, and even depression. You simply cannot afford to let your brain or body suffer if you have workout-related goals to meet, milestones to cross, and so on.

It's also no secret that malnutrition can harm you in ways that are considered critical to your health in the long run. Undernutrition, for example, can lead to obesity and heart disease later in life. Although you may not notice these diseases right away, the underlying changes in your body will orchestrate you down the path of damage. A good example of such changes is your metabolism, which will be drastically altered if you are undernourished. You can't expect anything good to come out of your workout routine when your body is being harmed in the worst way possible. So, unless organ failure is a long-term goal, you should think carefully about what you put into your body.

FOOD AND HIIT

Your body should get the food it needs to operate while you're exercising before you start working out—ideally, one to three hours before. Carbohydrates and protein should make up the majority of this.

Because carbohydrates burn quickly, they are deemed more important in this case. In other words, they provide a quick source of energy. Yes, carbs have a bad rep in the workout world, but it's a little-known fact that they're the best kind of resource for providing your body with enough fuel. Bananas, peanut butter toasts, and Greek yogurt are some of the most popular pre-workout foods among regular exercisers. There are probably more combinations out there, but as long as your body gets the right amount of energy from what you eat, you'll be fine.

When it comes to carbohydrates, keep in mind that not all carbs have the same effect on your body. Simple carbohydrates and complex carbohydrates are the two types of carbohydrates. Simple carbs are carbs that are easily broken down and absorbed, for an easy comparison between the two. Because quick absorption is a result of rapid digestion, it's safe to assume that simple carbohydrates are digested more quickly. Fruit juice concentrate, white bread, and milk are examples of simple carbohydrates. Complex carbs, on the other hand, are a different story. These carbs, as you may have guessed, take a long time to break down. They endure longer within your body, providing a steady supply of energy. On the cover, it appears that complex carbs are the way to go for better workout results. However, you don't want to find yourself in a scenario where your body is left behind.

Pre-workout meals should include a well-balanced mix of simple and complex carbohydrates for balance.

Let us now turn our attention to protein. Is it true that carbs are all you need before a workout? No, that is not the case. Protein is just as important for the post-workout phase of your body as carbs are for the pre-workout phase. Because protein is essential for recovery and because HIIT may cause minor muscle injury, your bloodstream should be stocked with enough protein to leap into action as soon as you leave the gym. It's good to incorporate some protein in your pre-workout meal, but not to the point where you feel too full to exercise afterwards. If you're going to have a protein-rich meal, it's best to avoid doing so shortly before your workout. Protein, unlike carbohydrates, takes longer to digest.

Your meal should be timed to coincide with the amount of time until you start your workout. When you just have a few minutes to spare, it's never a smart idea to consume anything that won't be digested in that time. This is why sports drinks exist for athletes who want to gain energy quickly without having to worry about the details. Water is one of the other essentials that your body requires prior to, during, and after your workout. In the realm of workouts, hydration is sometimes forgotten. It should come as no surprise that optimal hydration is responsible for a slew of little details that add up to a big influence on your exercise. Your body will sweat throughout your exercise, which will cause you to lose water. To avoid dehydration during your workout, make sure you have enough water in your tank.

Chapter Six

MANAGEIT: SLEEP, STRESS, & ANXIETY

Sleep, stress, and anxiety all go hand in hand, which few people realize. Your body was created to function in a cause-and-effect manner. In some ways, diet, sleep, stress, and exercise are intertwined. When one of the screws loosens, it affects the rest of the assembly. I didn't realize the interconnection between all of these different aspects that contributed to my well-being when I was a beginner in my early CrossFit days. To tell you the truth, I can't recall the last time I wasn't engrossed in a multitude of activities. Life has turned into a full-fledged race ever since my professional life entered the picture. Thinking that I could 'fit' my workout goals into my daily schedule was a rookie mistake I made back in the day. Working out isn't something you can throw into a suitcase and take with you wherever you go. It's a way of life that necessitates a high level of commitment.

As should be obvious by now, if you think you can save time by cutting down on your sleep and using it to exercise, you'll lose in both areas. If you don't put in the necessary effort into each criterion, the least-focused criteria are likely to have an impact on other aspects of your life. I was so desperate to meet my goals when I first started working out that I thought it would be a GREAT idea to sacrifice my sleep in order to train. Skipping a day was something I despised. "Well, I guess I'll just do it tomorrow," I didn't enjoy being the guy who said. I considered it a personal challenge. It was hurtful to me. I didn't get very far with that strategy, unsurprisingly. It wasn't supposed to happen like this. As a result, I became extremely stressed.

It's all the more dangerous for people like me who aren't willing to take a step back in life. It took a long time for me to realize I was causing myself harm. For everyone, it doesn't have to be like this. Keep in mind that your body does not communicate with you through language. Instead, it sends signals to your brain. When trying to figure out if your body is trying to show signs of fatigue, exhaustion, inability to concentrate, and so on, it's best to think about what went wrong during the day. Resolving the issue in this manner can significantly reduce your anxiety.

I'd also like to point out that, of all the points made here, getting enough sleep is by far the most important thing you can do to keep your CrossFit journey from becoming a disaster. So many different aspects of your daily life are accounted for by sleep. Sleep management entails stress reduction. Managing stress entails attending to the overall state of your body. It's all coming together. Either you do everything correctly or you leave something out, and everything goes wrong. Taking time for yourself to manage your sleep and stress will help you stay on track to meet your fitness goals. THE LIFESAVER IS SLEEP

Sleep is just as important as physical activity and a healthy diet. Many of the issues that your body may encounter can be solved by sleeping. Your body, like electronics, requires periodic recharge. When you sleep, your body begins to regenerate. It aids in the healing of an injury. It refreshes you when you are tired. Sleep can help you overcome a variety of problems. The advantages of sleeping could be the subject of a separate book. That is roughly the extent of the gains. Unfortunately, people you meet along your CrossFit journey will focus on how you should exercise rather than what you should do when you aren't exercising. Rest isn't a taboo subject, despite appearances to the contrary. It's perfectly acceptable to set aside time to unwind.

Sleep relaxes the brain, allowing it to function at its maximum capacity. As a result, your focus and productivity will improve. Sleep is also important for staying fit. Over the years, a number of studies have suggested that people with irregular sleeping patterns are more likely to gain weight. You might wonder, what's the connection. Well, poor sleeping patterns go hand in hand with poor life decisions. It pushes a person to think irrationally, causing him or her to become careless about weight. Speaking of weight, sleep also promotes the regulation of calories within your body. In other words, how your body processes the food that you consume will become more efficient when you have received an adequate amount of sleep.

Sleep is also linked to the prevention of certain diseases that may show up in the long run. One of the main organs that get affected by sleep deprivation is your heart. People who have irregular sleeping patterns also suffer from mental health issues such as depression, and studies indicate that sleep actually aids in the betterment of your mental health. Since you already know that sleeping helps you recover, it is no surprise that sleeping adequately can boost the immune system. So, at times when you are suffering from an infection or any other type of mild infection, sleeping will promote the recovery of that by facilitating regeneration and also by lowering any inflammation that may exist inside your body.

Sleep even allows the body to heal, save energy, and repair and rebuild the muscles that have been used during exercise. One of the key causes for poor exercise performance is perceived commitment rather than real physiological changes in the muscles and cardiovascular system. To power the workouts, your body uses glycogen, which is stored as energy in the muscles. When your glycogen stores are depleted, you'll begin to feel tired, and it's best you refuel yourself on sleep in order to be in a good shape for subsequent workouts.

The body also releases growth hormones when we get enough good-quality sleep, which aid in the development of lean muscle and the recovery of our bodies after a strenuous workout.

Given all of the above, it comes as no surprise that sleep is, by every meaning of the phrase, a major stress reducer. We already know about how it regenerates the body, strengthens the immune system, regulates your moods, stabilizes your metabolic system, enhances your concentration, and so much more. All of these attributes, altogether, help in the reduction of your stress.

EATING HABITS

Studies show that there is an inverse relationship between healthy eating and sleep. When people are sleep-deprived, they tend to crave more unhealthy foods, which usually leads to\s

weight gain. Ghrelin and leptin, two neurotransmitters that tell our brain when to eat calories, are affected by sleep deprivation. People who don't get enough sleep are more likely to crave high- calorie foods. Sleep deprivation has been attributed to a greater waist circumference and a higher risk of obesity. There was a case in which researchers interviewed 5,000 adults on how much they ate and how much sleep they got. They found that adults who slept for at least six hours a night weighed less than those who slept for fewer hours.

Simultaneously, throughout the day, consuming less fiber, more saturated fat, and more sugar is related to lighter, less restorative sleep. High-carbohydrate, high-glycemic-index meals can also impact energy levels and sleep quality. It's common knowledge that high-carbohydrate meals will make you feel drowsy. High-carbohydrate meals can also make it difficult to get a good night's sleep. It's best not to eat large meals late at night. If you're going to eat something substantial, do it in the middle of the day. You'll be less likely to retain the extra calories as fat because you'll have more time to burn them off, and you'll have less heartburn. In your CrossFit journey, you can't afford to compromise your sleeping or eating habits.

Now, how does it all come together? You see, your body needs a bit of everything. Stress, hunger, and sleep are all related, and affecting one of these will synonymously have an effect on the rest. These three things work in a full circle. For instance, lack of sleep may have an effect on a person's potential food decisions. Bad food decisions can lead to anxiety. Many who do not get enough sleep make bad decisions and suffer from high anxiety, consequently mashing up stress, diet, and sleep together. This turns into a vicious cycle that keeps repeating itself endlessly, with poor food choices and anxiety leading to poor sleep, which leads to more poor food choices and anxiety subsequently. Ultimately, your health gets dragged in between.

READY, SET, RELAX

Soothing Baths

Submersion in water can relieve pain and inflammation while also calming the nervous system, lower stress/anxiety levels, and improve mood. Bath meditation incorporates the traditional benefits of meditation. With a hot bath, one can soothe sore muscles, create a calming environment, and indulge in a temporary sense of relief from stressors. Water has long been thought to have healing properties in most ancient cultures. The Japanese practice of "Sento," or public bathing, is similar to mindfulness in that it is used to cleanse both the body and the mind. Just how your skin releases endorphins in response to feeling the sun, your skin releases endorphins in response to soothing warm water. Spare 15 minutes in your average day to just sit back, relax, and focus on the sensation of a warm bath. It'll do wonders for your CrossFit journey.

HE PSYCHOLOGICAL TRIANGLE

With all that said, it's a given that stress, anxiety, and sleep correlate with each other at all times. If one of them takes a hit, the others will show their effects. To maintain a stable CrossFit routine, one must pay attention to all three aspects equally. Whenever you start to feel that you're lacking in one of those areas, it should be treated before the effect expands and starts affecting the other areas. The best course to avoid getting stuck in that trap is to keep a check on how your body is responding to daily activity. As soon as you realize that you're not doing your 100 percent, start investigating the root cause of the problem and don't rule out the possibility that it could be any of these three.

Chapter Seven

FUELUP: CROSS FIT EAT INGGUIDE LINES

GETTING STARTED

Now, it's time to talk about the dietary portion of your CrossFit journey, which is just as essential—if not more so—as your workout routine. When innovative training and good nutrition are combined, the human body is capable of achieving exceptional results. Conversely, if your diet isn't in order, even the most intense CrossFit workouts won't help you lose weight, add muscle, or get fitter. Diet has a substantial influence on how you look and feel in the gym, particularly when it comes to appearance. However, diet is a complex topic, and much of what is available online is written with ulterior motives in mind, such as "Sign up for my nutrition therapy!" Although there's nothing wrong with that, it can make it challenging to sort through the details. We'll do away with all that in this book.

My aim is to help you cover all of your bases and to educate you about the fundamentals of a successful CrossFit diet; to give you an idea of where to begin, to show you how to lose weight and build strength, and to provide you with the necessary tools. The reality is that your diet is unique to you. Do not go in and expect to see results in days or even weeks. If someone tells you a secret formula for how to get in shape while defining a certain amount of time, it's just a load of rubbish. No two bodies are one hundred percent the same. There will always be things that will vary across different individuals. If you and I train the same exact way simultaneously, it does not guarantee that our outcomes would be the same. You'll have to experiment to see what works best for you. It takes time, but it's the best investment you can make in your health and fitness journey.

Understanding Macronutrients

Macronutrients are the fundamental components of all human foods. It's vital for a CrossFitter to have a balanced macronutrient intake to fuel their efforts and recover properly. They can be divided into 3 groups: protein, carbohydrates, and fats. To break it down scientifically, a gram of protein or starch has four calories, while a gram of fat has nine. Proteins aid in the growth of muscle and hair, as well as the regulation of many bodily functions. Carbs have a poor rep in the diet world. If you've ever followed a low-carb diet, you're probably used to hating them. But they're not all that bad because, on the flip side of the coin, carbohydrates fuel our efforts. Carbs are converted into glucose by the liver, which provides us with the energy to complete tasks. Managing your carbohydrate intake by smart sources and careful monitoring will help you get the most out of this amazing success tool. And lastly, about fats, well, they

keep our nervous system stable by regulating a variety of hormonal processes in our bodies.

Understanding Micronutrients

Now, what are micronutrients? They are the highly crucial vitamins and minerals that a healthy body needs to function properly. They're necessary for disease prevention, growth, and well-being. Vitamin A, iron, iodine, and zinc are some examples. Iron deficiency, for example, can impair cognitive and motor development. The majority of micronutrients can be obtained by consuming a diet rich in lean meats, vegetables, and fruits. Micronutrients are needed in smaller quantities than macronutrients. That's why they're referred to as "micro". Humans must receive micronutrients from food because, for the most part, the body is unable to produce vitamins and minerals. Minerals are inorganic substances that reside in soil or water and cannot be broken down. On the other hand, vitamins are organic compounds produced by plants and animals and can be degraded by fire, acid, or air.

TYPES OF CROSSFIT DIETS

When it comes to discovering the right CrossFit diet, the most important thing to consider is your fitness goal. Are you attempting to lose or gain weight? Maybe all you want to do is keep up with the Joneses? The reality is that CrossFit dieting is like clothing, and no one size is going to fit everybody. Some people do CrossFit to lose weight, others to add strength, and others to simply remain healthy. Regardless of why you're doing CrossFit, you can choose a diet that suits you and that you can stick to in the long run. The safest diet is one that can be maintained over time. However, there are still some factors to remember, such as the amount of energy you'll need to complete your workouts. With that said, in retrospect, CrossFit has promoted a few nutritional approaches: the Zone diet, the Paleo diet, and the Ketogenic diet are a few of the most common.

Zone Diet

So, what exactly is the Zone diet? For starters, it's a diet that uses block counting and a healthy macro split (30/30/40) to ensure you eat foods that hold you in a good "zone" for

success. It is designed to minimize inflammation and regulate hormones. The Zone diet requires you to eat on a schedule, beginning one hour after you wake up and continuing every three to four hours to maintain your energy level. On the Zone diet, you can consume most foods, but whole foods are better to avoid because they are easier to balance. The Zone diet's equivalent of portions is 'blocks', making this plan somewhat close to macro monitoring. The Zone plan does have one caveat. The suggested regular "bars" for women and men are 11 and 14 respectively. This advice is very restrictive when you do the math. Although you can lose weight on this diet, it is not very sustainable.

TO EAT OR NOT TO EAT

Let's talk about vilifying foods for a minute before we move on. As a CrossFit competitor, it's critical to emphasize nutrition, but it's also critical not to be too restrictive. Make an effort to cultivate a positive attitude toward food. Can eating Grandma's brown bread or sharing a few drinks with your best buddies help you get through your CrossFit workout? Maybe not. Will skipping social activities and obsessing about food decisions have a negative impact on your mental health? Without a doubt. Consider partnering with a wellness coach to help you achieve your goals without compromising your quality of life if you're having trouble finding it. I've said this before, and I'll say it again, you are what you eat. You can't expect to be dosing on sugary

sodas, fried chicken, and all the other sorts of 'junk' and still have goals for getting in shape. One of these things has to go.

Food to Avoid

It's important to strike a balance, but consuming highly processed foods on a daily basis can make it difficult to meet your fitness goals. Your body needs "clean" fuel while you are setting new personal records in the gym and working hard. Ensure that your diet consists of foods that are easily digestible, rich in nutrients, and can be converted rapidly without stressing your stomach and causing inflammation. As a general rule, limit processed foods, concentrate on lean protein and healthy fats, and replace the low-carb mindset with a smart-carb mindset. Feed it sparingly if it comes from a bag or contains ingredients you can't pronounce. You may also set aside less-than-ideal options for a "cheat meal." Your fitness should come before the social temptation that says, "It's just this once."

How to Put a Meal Plan Together

We've talked about your diet and CrossFit goals in broad terms up to this stage. Now, let's go through a more "step-by-step" approach for you to understand how to get started with your meal plan if you haven't done it before.

To kick things off, find out your basal metabolic rate (BMR) and activity level by doing some online research. Since your BMR just considers how many calories you burn at rest, don't forget to consider your activity rate. If you've determined your protein needs, for example, estimate how much real food (Paleo or Zone approved) you'll need to meet them. For instance, what do 150 grams of protein in lean ground turkey and chicken breast look like on a daily basis? Building long-term habits takes time. One of the reasons fad diets fail is that they promote an all- or-nothing mentality. Perhaps you only have one or two days this week that are suitable for your new meal schedule. It will take some time for you to develop the habit of grocery shopping and meal preparation. From a glass-half-full perspective, you have now figured out what you will be eating for 2 out of 7 days in a week. Appreciate the progress.

Starting with lean meat choices, fruit, and vegetables as building blocks is a good idea, even if you don't want to adopt a diet plan. You can then add other healthy options, including rice, potatoes, and legumes, to round out your meal. There are a plethora of meal preparation guides and recipes available on the internet. To begin, gather all of your Tupperware and prepare your Crockpot for fast cooking. Aim for 1-2 weeks' worth of meal preps, and cook a little extra so you have leftovers in the fridge. If necessary, don't be afraid to take shortcuts. For those hectic days, buying roasted chicken and pre-cut vegetables from the supermarket is perfectly appropriate. When life doesn't go as planned, these shortcuts can come in more handy and productive than a quick trip to the nearest drive-through.

Chapter Eight

TEN MOST COMMONIN JURIESIN CROSS FIT

Whatever outdoor activity you pick, some hitches and mishaps are inevitable. Crossfit isn't any different. You are incorrect if you believe you will be immune to mishaps that occur while others exercise. It's just that you can never be too safe. Despite how effective CrossFit is, health care experts often warn their patients about some of the most prevalent injuries and diseases linked with it. If people wish to maximize the potential of this program and enjoy the physical advantages that come with it, they need protect themselves against these hazards.

Being inside a gym or training facility might be scary, particularly if you get the impression that everyone is watching at you. Some of us are unconcerned with our surroundings, but the majority are. We not only keep an eye on our surroundings, but we also make it a personal challenge to perform our best. To be honest, I don't see anything wrong with it. I'll confess that I was one of those men who constantly tried to outdo the man next to me on the treadmill—in good spirit, of course. But, in such tense situations, we frequently miss our bodies' warning indications. We may go in and do this every day until it becomes second nature. Our bodies will change throughout time. It deteriorates, wears down, and needs maintenance. As a result, we must continually keep an eye out for any new pain or signs of discomfort.

BEWARE OF THE FOLLOWING INJURIES

CrossFit is more than simply a workout. It's a way of life that includes endurance-testing workouts that build muscle, burn fat, and improve conditioning. Because CrossFit includes weight lifting, aerobics, running, and gymnastics, it is not for the faint of heart. When it comes to hitting the local box, it's vital to train carefully in order to get the greatest outcomes. CrossFit exercises are a sort of high-intensity interval training that burns calories, improves agility, and boosts strength, therefore it should come as no surprise that high intensity comes with high danger. In this case, studying what might damage you will provide you with the information and understanding necessary to avoid it.

Tendonitis in the Achilles tendon

As the name indicates, this is an injury involving the tendons and the Achilles heel. Achilles tendonitis is caused by overuse of the tendon at the back of your heel. The Achilles tendon links the calf muscle to the heel bone. If you overwork and strain your feet, you may have soreness, stiffness, edema, and difficulty bending them. The best approaches to prevent Achilles tendinitis are to wear good footwear, extend the ankle correctly, and attend at least one reflexology treatment per month. Apart from that, there's a disorder called Plantar Fasciitis, which produces pain at the bottom of your foot rather than the rear of your ankle. If this injury is not addressed, the tendon may be blown out, necessitating surgery. People who have sustained this injury must take time off before returning to their regular routine to enable the damage to heal. If you fall into this group, you should do heel lifts after cooling the tendon to maintain it loose and supple. Alternatively, you might wait until it has completely healed before applying any pressure.

Neck injuries are common.

Because CrossFit is built on several Olympic-style moves, you'll spend a lot of time raising a barbell above your head or supporting a barbell around your traps. Lifting too much weight or falling a barbell on your neck may injure your cervical spine, resulting in extreme agony and even paralysis. We utilize our necks for a lot more movement than you would realize in CrossFit. Pull-ups (chin over bar), Olympic lifts (eyes straight ahead), wall balls (looking up), and burpees are just a few. Squats, deadlifts, jump ropes, and shoulder presses are among the less well-known exercises. Regardless, if we consider this, we may lessen the risks of stiffness and imbalance. Excessive movement in the non-stiff portions might lead to considerable stiffness and discomfort if we take the stiffness and imbalances we build throughout the day and work out with routines that demand neck motion. As a result, be conscious of how your body feels at all times.

Knee Pain in the Forehead

Knees are one of the most injured body areas in CrossFit clubs. Knee discomfort is so common that most individuals just ignore it and continue about their daily lives. Knee discomfort is most often caused by overuse and strain, but it may sometimes signify a more serious injury such as a dislocation or rupture. Stay away from high-impact exercises that put a lot of pressure on your knees if you have knee discomfort. You may freeze your knees, limit their physical impact, and stretch to keep them limber if you have slight discomfort or inflammation. You should visit a doctor if the swelling or deformity continues. People with this illness should cease putting pressure on their knees if the knee cap is swollen or dislocated.

PRECAUTIONS

Listening to your own body is perhaps the most important measure you can take. It doesn't get much safer. Pay attention to the noises it makes, the pain messages it transmits, and the differences between yesterday and today. This isn't to say that you should give up as soon as you hear a crack. Simply said, if you hear one too many, don't turn a deaf ear. During a typical CrossFit workout, a typical CrossFit competitor will experience some discomfort. Nobody said it would be easy. It's only a matter of educating oneself on what may go wrong. After that, take all of your ideas and play it safe.

Chapter Nine

FIVE MOST COMMON PAIN COMPLAINTS

The plethora of seemingly similar pain complaints that many CrossFit athletes make from time to time are something that many CrossFit athletes have in common. In this respect, I was no exception. Despite this commonality, it's critical that we understand why we're in pain so that we can distinguish between a minor ache and a serious underlying problem. It's possible that not knowing can hide an impending injury. My gym buddy used to brag about how heavy he could lift all the time. If I'm being completely honest, he mostly followed through on his promises. He did, however, occasionally complain (or rather boast) about his ability to overcome his pain. I'm not sure if it was the adrenaline or if he was simply distracted, but the guy dropped a heavy barbell flat on the floor one day, drawing everyone's attention. He tore his muscle and was out of commission for several months as a result. Don't be the guy who makes that mistake.

Irritation

One of the most common complaints among athletes who squat and/or sit for extended periods of time is back pain. There is no way to avoid a movement like this in the CrossFit world. By doing the bare minimum, no escape strategy will prevent you from getting hurt. There isn't always a lot of room for the ball in the hip socket to "roll around" when you have a squeeze in your hip. The athlete's hip has rolled forward too far, and his tailbone has shifted over. Clearing some space is the best thing to do here. At this point, the jump bands are useful. We can use the band for more than just stretching muscles; we can use it to apply traction and detach two bones that are too close together if we use it correctly. During growth, they also fall forward faster because they have more weight in the front. The brain's attempt to keep the body straight can lead to musculature system imbalances. The feet and lower body muscles are ultimately responsible for preventing a person from collapsing face down on the ground. So, what are your options for dealing with the situation? The calf muscles must first be relaxed before they can be fully lengthened. In this case, the foam roller and a lacrosse/tennis ball are extremely useful.

Sensation of Fever

The plethora of seemingly similar pain complaints that many CrossFit athletes make from time to time are something that many CrossFit athletes have in common. In this respect, I was no exception. Despite this commonality, it's critical that we understand why we're in pain so that we can distinguish between a minor ache and a serious underlying problem. It's possible that not knowing can hide an impending injury. My gym buddy used to brag about how heavy he could lift all the time. If I'm being completely honest, he mostly followed through on his promises. He did, however, occasionally complain (or rather boast) about his ability to overcome his pain. I'm not sure if it was the adrenaline or if he was simply distracted, but the guy dropped a heavy barbell flat on the floor one day, drawing everyone's attention. He tore his muscle and was out of commission for several months as a result. Don't be the guy who makes that mistake.

Irritation

One of the most common complaints among athletes who squat and/or sit for extended periods of time is back pain. There is no way to avoid a movement like this in the CrossFit world. By doing the bare minimum, no escape strategy will prevent you from getting hurt. There isn't always a lot of room for the ball in the hip socket to "roll around" when you have a squeeze in your hip. The athlete's hip has rolled forward too far, and his tailbone has shifted over. Clearing some space is the best thing to do here. At this point, the jump bands are useful. We can use the band for more than just stretching muscles; we can use it to apply traction and detach two bones that are too close together if we use it correctly. During growth, they also fall forward faster because they have more weight in the front. The brain's attempt to keep the body straight can lead to musculature system imbalances. The feet and lower body muscles are ultimately responsible for preventing a person from collapsing face down on the ground. So, what are your options for dealing with the situation? The calf muscles must first be relaxed before they can be fully lengthened. In this case, the foam roller and a lacrosse/tennis ball are extremely useful.

Sensation of Fever

Chapter Ten

PREP YOUR BODY BEFORE YOUR WORKOUT

One of the most common misunderstandings (and errors) among new CrossFitters is that good results are proportional to speed. To put it another way, we believe we can complete a 45-minute workout in 25 minutes and reap the same benefits, which is completely untrue. Warm-up sessions are often neglected. Many of us ignore our bodies' signals and fail because we haven't prepared properly. Yes, you'll see posters in nearly every training center or gym encouraging you to go all out and lift the heaviest weights available. It's not impossible that you'll succeed, but if you want to do it effectively and safely, you'll need to prepare and discipline yourself. Take it from me: I used to be the type of guy who wanted to accomplish more in less time, which didn't always work out. It's important to recognize that training is about more than who sweats the most. It's an art form, a race in which the slowest runner wins.

STARTING AT THE BOTTOM

Where do we begin, then? What can you do to make yourself'ready'? It's not as easy as tying your laces and going to the gym. There's more to it than that. However, let's talk about CrossFit boxes when it comes to going to the gym. Boxes have sprung up all over the place as a result of the recent CrossFit boom, but not all of them are equal. If you haven't found your favorite box yet, check out a few others in your area or go with a friend to his or her favorite. Finally, You should work out in a gym that is designed for your safety and performance, with knowledgeable and enthusiastic instructors who will help you perfect your shape and technique. You'll also want to be surrounded by athletes who inspire and encourage you rather than making you feel inferior or obligated to compete at all times.

Competition, on the other hand, isn't necessarily a bad thing. Indeed, friendly competition can help you prepare to some extent. It instills in you a sense of urgency and a desire to succeed. Consider yourself the only one in the room who needs to get in shape. Do you think you'd be as motivated as he is? When it comes to your CrossFit journey, competition is a great motivator, but don't let it get out of hand. It's critical to stay focused on your personal objectives and why you're exercising in the first place. While having a more experienced CrossFitter as a coach can be beneficial, you should avoid comparing yourself to them, lest your attempt to outdo them lead to mistakes and accidents. Focusing on achieving your own #PersonalBest rather than trying to outdo someone else's will also give you more self-efficacy and long-term motivation.

And no, being surrounded by gym equipment does not automatically qualify you. Even if you have the best equipment available, learning how to use it is an important part of your preparation. Consider it more of a beast than a machine that you must tame and master. Just because a machine is efficient doesn't guarantee that your workout will be. With nothing more than what Mother Nature has provided you: your body, you can begin a successful workout journey. The most technologically advanced facilities and well-equipped gyms will only produce results if they are properly utilized on a daily basis. Spend time learning how to use these tools correctly to avoid accidents that could keep you out of work for an extended period of time.

MENTAL AND PHYSICAL PREPARATION WORKING IN CONJUNCTION

Even a strength and conditioning coach will almost certainly require the assistance of a psychological specialist in order to develop the ideal strategy and develop the necessary interventions for the best possible result. Your effort is a choice, and it necessitates both mental and physical input. Furthermore, your ability to concentrate is undeniably a mental factor with behavioral consequences. Positive feedback can help athletes improve their self-esteem and self-talk. Two examples of imagery or imagination that can boost an athlete's morale are visualizing a good lift before it occurs and imagining oneself better in the future. These are the small things that can make a big difference in your day-to-day life. Then there's music, which has long been used as a signal to adjust athlete strength levels in both competition and training situations in exercise and sport situations. Both physical and mental preparation are necessary for success. Working on the right combination of the two will yield the best results.

Don't even consider whether you'll win or lose. You'll only be distracted by the physical requirements of the job. Learn to ignore the factors over which you have no control, just as you should ignore the weather and terrain on a daily basis. Some things just happen that you can't control. Instead, concentrate on your abilities. During your workout, concentrate on the movements you need to make. Instead of visualizing the end result, break it down into individual steps and visualize each one. To move forward, your mind requires encouragement, and the best kind comes from within. Many talented athletes use visualization to prepare for a professional game. They create scenarios in their heads and plan how to deal with them. It aids in their mental preparation. Preparing for a competition or a training session by telling yourself a thoughtful and purposeful story will help you respond quickly whenever necessary. Set yourself up for success by approaching the situation with a positive attitude. Recognize your typical response to various stressors and develop a strategy to deal with them. Keep a journal handy to jot down your thoughts if it helps. You'll also be able to review and learn from the thought patterns you've recorded. To get pumped up, some people prefer fast-paced music. Others rely on the encouragement of their friends or fans to succeed. Some people prefer to meditate or relax in a quiet environment while listening to soothing music. Choose the best form for you and use it!

Keep in mind that your mental and physical well-being are intertwined. If one of them isn't in good shape, the other will suffer. Perhaps the most powerful link between mental and physical fitness exists here. Without putting forth the necessary effort, results are rarely obtained. "Becoming more centered, optimistic, and resilient" is a rough translation of "getting bigger, faster, and stronger" in this context. All six descriptors are correct, but only after the necessary movements, exercises, and activities have been improved. In a nutshell, mental strength is required for physical strength to exist. As a result, in addition to a physical plan, you should also have a mental plan in place, all while sticking to a strategic schedule.

WARM-UPS ARE VERY IMPORTANT

Even though they won't help you lose weight or gain muscle, warm-ups are necessary for a successful workout. People will warm up and stretch before even thinking about running or using the gym's machines. However, most people only spend 15 to 20 minutes warming up on a treadmill or stationary bike. Although most fitness experts agree that "this is better than nothing," warming up for a high-intensity CrossFit session requires more than a quick warm-up. Stretches and hip/leg extensions, trunk/hip extensions and flexions, as well as pushing and pulling movements, should all be included in your pre-workout warm-ups. But first, what is the significance of warm-ups?

Flexibility

Stretching increases blood flow to your muscles and allows your body to become more flexible in the short and long term, both of which are beneficial when it comes to properly performing a workout. Stretch only after you've completed the rest of your warm-up, as stretching before your muscles are warm enough can lead to injury. Your muscles will feel less tense, and your posture will improve dramatically if done correctly. Above all, stretching increases body flexibility, which helps to reduce the risk of injury during a strenuous workout.

Heavy-Duty Compliant

Machines can help you build muscle, but you shouldn't use them before loosening your joints. Warming up ensures that both your body and mind are ready to handle exercise equipment, reducing your risk of injury. Not only should you warm up before your workout, but you should also make sure you have the right equipment for the workouts you'll be doing. Accessories such as resistance bands, palm guards, and other similar items will benefit CrossFit.

GET THE GLASS AND FILL IT UP.

One of the many prerequisites for achieving your workout goals is to adopt the right mindset that will facilitate greater progress and results, in addition to physically preparing your body. Learning a new skill takes time and dedication. Learning to play a sport or an instrument can be frustrating at times, especially when things don't go as planned. However, as they say, practice makes perfect, so mentally prepare yourself for the practice ahead of time.

0-1

Chapter Eleven

MINDSET: CROSS FIT SUCCESS

Negativity has no place in the CrossFit world. You can't afford to be distracted by your own flaws or confusion when putting in such a significant amount of effort. To be at the top of your game, you must identify and eliminate all negative emotions that can harm you directly or indirectly. To be successful at CrossFit, you must adopt the right mindset.

SELF-SABOTAGE

Failure aversion

To begin, you must determine whether or not you are afraid of failing. The answer to this question, if you're honest with yourself, will reveal both the source of your fear and the first step toward overcoming it. Fear of failure can be fueled by a variety of factors, such as the desire not to disappoint friends, family, coaches, or anyone else who is invested in your success. Athletes devote countless hours to training, and the more dedicated they are, the more assistance they will require from their support network. You could be putting a lot of pressure on yourself to succeed without even realizing it. Others are afraid of failing because they have unrealistic expectations of themselves, seek external recognition, or fear losing their competitive advantage. Identifying the source of your negative attitude toward failure, whatever the reason, is essential to achieving your goals.

People become stressed or anxious when they focus on something they have no control over. By assisting people in focusing on what they can control, it provides a sense of certainty and trust. The end result in education and sports can often conceal flaws. Young people may believe that everything is fine after receiving a good grade or winning their most recent competition. A poor grade or a loss, on the other hand, casts a pall over everything. Anxiety, tension, and a lowered sense of self-worth can all result from this type of black-and-white thinking. Your attitude, effort, and what you've learned are better indicators, and these are more likely to lead to good grades and success. Failure in and of itself isn't dangerous. It's just a way to get recommendations for where you are right now. People are worried about the negative consequences they anticipate. Don't let hypothetical concerns detract from what you've accomplished in the real world.

Continuous Negativity Self-doubt

Negative self-talk is one of the most harmful things we can do, and while we may not realize it at the time, it has significant mental and physical consequences. At some point in our lives, almost all of us have battled the nagging voice in our heads. You know the one... the one that tells you you're not good enough, you'll never change, you'll never achieve your goals. We've all been there, but the truth is that our cynical inner voice isn't telling us the truth. Recognize that you're doing it in the first place before you try to stop. How many times have you told yourself, "I can't finish this exercise," "I'm dying!" or "I don't want to do this any longer!"?

You will notice a significant improvement in your performance if you begin to notice when those thoughts enter your mind and work to replace them with positive mantras on a regular basis. Tell yourself, "I can," rather than "I can't." Replace the nagging voice of dread with an uplifting voice that says, "I can do this." when you're faced with three sets of burpees. Begin to recognize when you're engaging in negative self-talk so you can work on changing it. You're more likely to give up or never try if you believe you won't be able to complete the punishing 20-minute assault-bike session or squat a heavyweight. Negative self-talk has no place in the gym, because fitness is so much about believing in yourself, trying new things, and never giving up. Maintain a positive mindset while exercising.

The inability to concentrate

What you put your attention on grows in power. Negative thoughts can take away your ability to focus on your CrossFit goals. What you concentrate on determines the parts of your brain that burn, wire, and reinforce. Permanent associations are formed when those parts of the brain turn on and the neurons begin to fire, reinforcing memories and influencing future brain focus. The issue is that while it is natural to think about the negative, it is also natural to overlook the positive. After a day of great conversation, wonderful people, and enriching experiences, it's not uncommon for your mind to become fixated on one argument. To make room for focusing on the things that really matter, you need to clear out your inner negativity.

Surprisingly

TAKE THE FOLLOWING MEASURES:

Keep an eye on the numbers

A fitness tracker can help you by providing useful data that allows you to see what you've accomplished, as well as keeping track of your health and fitness records, progress, and allowing you to connect with others. All of these things will assist you in staying on track and focused. You're more likely to push yourself harder when you see their levels of activity. It also helps you move forward in your fitness journey.

Overall, fitness trackers will encourage you to exercise more and help you improve your workout results. They'll show you numbers and figures that correspond to what you did in the training center. You'll develop a natural desire to do more in this manner.

When you have company, it's even better. One of the most accurate predictors of fitness success is the availability of assistance. When people feel supported, they are more likely to follow through on their health goals and achieve better results. You can also keep your motivation by inviting your friends, coworkers, or gym buddies to train with you and track data together. The ability to communicate with others on a social, competitive, and supportive level expands your tracker's potential. The ability to sync your fitness tracker with others, even if they don't have the same tracker as you, is a game-changer in terms of staying connected and accountable. You can also connect multiple devices and track data from a variety of sources to keep track of your health and fitness. This knowledge would be extremely beneficial to your future health.

Seek Feedback

More often than not, negative motivation helps prevent emotional pain, while positive motivation follows emotional pleasure. In other words, we won't act until the pain of not acting outweighs the pain of acting and vice versa. Emotional motivation, on the other hand, is the most effective form of motivation. This is sometimes referred to as feedback. Positive reinforcement increases our self-esteem and sense of well-being, motivating us to replicate the behavior that caused these feelings. It keeps you up for 24 hours straight, allowing you to finish a passion project without looking at the clock. You ought to seek positive feedback about what you're trying to achieve from those you trust. It's important to share what you do in order to stay engaged.

Read More

Reading has long been a common pastime enjoyed by people of all ages. Reading books has

the power to change your brain — and your body. Regular reading enhances memory capacity by giving your brain a healthy workout, just as physical exercise does for your cardiovascular system. According to studies, a person's memory and brain capacity decrease with age, but daily reading can help delay the transition and keep minds sharper for longer. It has been discovered that repeated brain exercise can reduce mental deterioration by 32 percent . Nonfiction self-help books can teach you techniques that can help you overcome symptoms, while fiction can encourage you to briefly escape your own life and become caught up in the imaginary experiences of the characters, which ultimately can reduce symptoms of depression. It is highly recommended to people who work out to read self-developmental books for their own betterment.

Your Pace, Your Way

Finally, let's shed some light on how setting your own pace can save you from a lot of unnecessary grief. You know you need a workout strategy, you know you need a meal plan, and you also know what to avoid to stay determined. The thing is, all of your efforts can still go to waste if you are too obsessed with what a certain individual is achieving. This certain individual could be a friend, someone who works with you, or, quite simply, another guy in the same training center. You need to stay focused on yourself and yourself only. This is the biggest favor one can do for himself or herself. Set your own pace for your goals, and walk that path. Don't worry if others have done the same in less time. Quite frankly, there will always be someone who's better than you, no matter what you do. You will always hear about someone who did something that you haven't done. Ignore that, and try to be the most authentic version of yourself.

CPSIA information can be obtained
at www.ICGtesting.com
Printed in the USA
LVHW050817010422
714993LV00007B/223

ISBN 978-1-80438-514-2

PALEO

RECIPES WITH SLOW COOKER

Enjoy Your Paleo Dishes Without The Work

KEVIN M. WHITE